My first vocabulary

PRICE STERN SLOAN LIMITED, NORTHAMPTON, ENGLAND

The fun way to bring learning to life

This book is part of the **Questron** system, which offers children a unique aid to learning and endless hours of challenging entertainment.

The **Questron** Electronic Answer Wand uses a microchip to sense correct and incorrect answers with ''right'' or ''wrong'' sounds and lights. Victory sounds and lights reward the user when particular sets of questions or games are completed. Powered by a nine-volt alkaline battery, which is activated only when the wand is pressed on a page, **Questron** should have an exceptionally long life. The **Questron** Electronic Answer Wand can be used with any book in the **Questron** series.

A note to parents...

With **Questron**, right or wrong answers are indicated instantly and can be tried over and over again to reinforce learning and improve skills. Children need not be restricted to the books designated for their age group, as interests and rates of development vary widely. Also, within many of the books, certain pages are designed for the older end of the age group and will provide a stimulating challenge to younger children.

Many activities are designed at different levels. For example, the child can select an answer by recognizing a letter or by reading an entire word. The activities for pre-readers and early readers are intended to be used with parental assistance. Interaction with parents or older children will stimulate the learning experience.

Printed in Great Britain by
Purnell Book Production Limited
Member of the BPCC Group

How to start Questron®

Hold **Questron** at this angle and press the activator button firmly on the page.

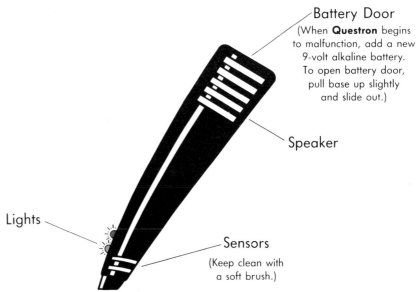

Battery Door
(When **Questron** begins to malfunction, add a new 9-volt alkaline battery. To open battery door, pull base up slightly and slide out.)

Speaker

Lights

Sensors
(Keep clean with a soft brush.)

How to use Questron®

Press

Press **Questron** firmly on the shape below, then lift it off.

Track

Press **Questron** down on "Start" and keep it pressed down as you move to "Finish".

Start

Finish

Right and wrong with Questron®

Press **Questron** on the square.

See the green light and hear the sound. This green light and sound say "You are correct".

Press **Questron** on the triangle.

The red light and sound say "Try again". Lift **Questron** off the page and wait for the sound to stop.

Press **Questron** on the circle.

Hear the victory sound. Don't be dazzled by the flashing lights. You deserve them.

High Flying Balloons

Press **Questron** on the colour word that matches each balloon.

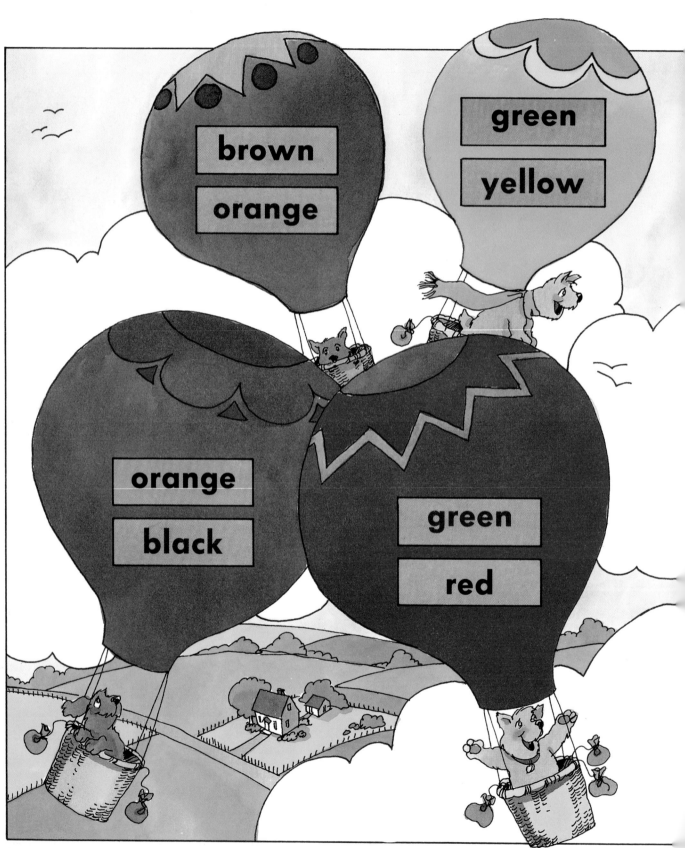

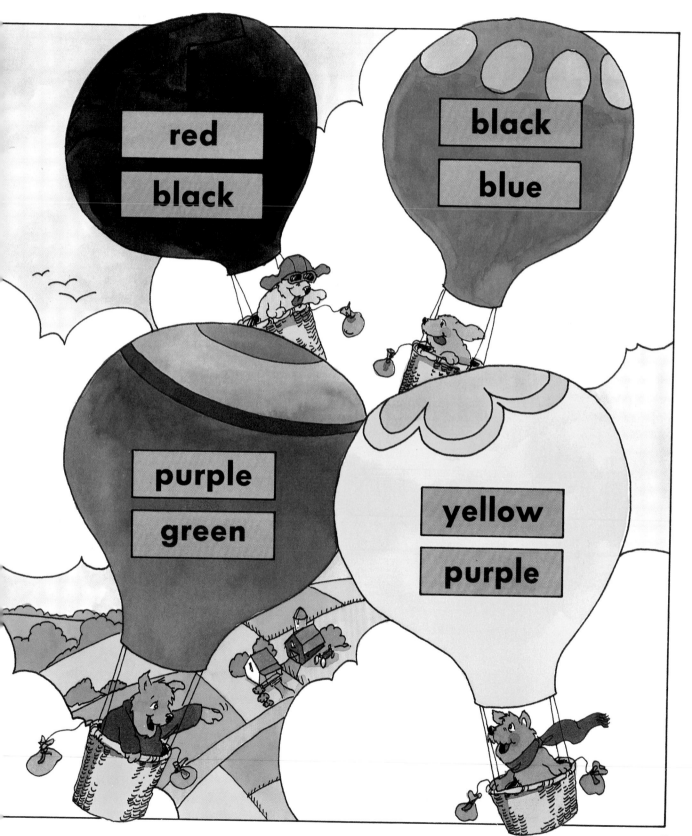

Colours and Crayons

What colours are the crayons? Track **Questron** on the colour word that matches each crayon. Start on the ★.

★	yellow	purple	orange
	yellow	yellow	green
	brown	yellow	yellow

★	red	blue	orange
	red	red	red
	green	brown	black

★	blue	blue	black
	brown	blue	blue
	yellow	green	purple

★	purple	purple	yellow
	blue	purple	green
	red	purple	purple

★	orange	orange	blue
	green	orange	purple
	yellow	orange	orange

★	green	orange	blue
	green	green	purple
	yellow	green	green

★	brown	yellow	green
	brown	brown	brown
	orange	blue	yellow

Shape Words

Press **Questron** on the shape that matches the word in each row.

circle	●	▬	▲
square	▲	●	■
triangle	●	▲	▬
oval	⬭	▬	◆
rectangle	▬	●	▲
diamond	◆	⬭	●

More Shape Words

Press **Questron** on the word that matches each shape.

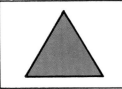 | **triangle** | **circle** | **square**

 | **rectangle** | **triangle** | **circle**

 | **diamond** | **square** | **triangle**

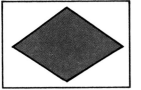 | **square** | **circle** | **diamond**

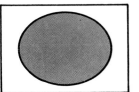 | **oval** | **circle** | **square**

 | **square** | **rectangle** | **oval**

All Aboard!

Look at the picture.
Press **Questron** on the correct answers.

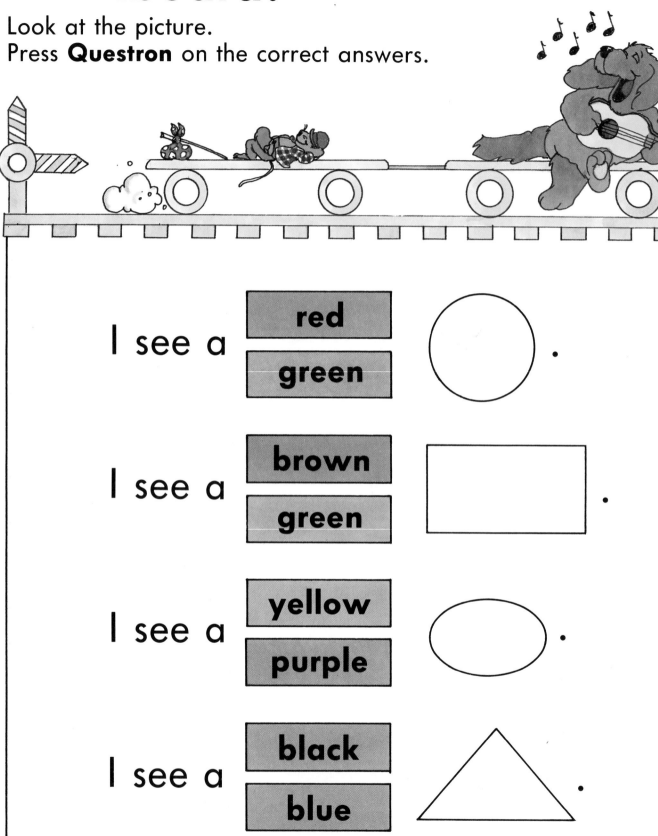

I see a | red / green | ◯ .

I see a | brown / green | ▭ .

I see a | yellow / purple | ⬭ .

I see a | black / blue | △ .

I see a blue **triangle** / **square** .

I see a red **diamond** / **circle** .

I see a brown **oval** / **square** .

I see a black **diamond** / **triangle** .

The Amazing Counting Dog

Track **Questron** on the path with number words that match the numbers. Start on the ★.

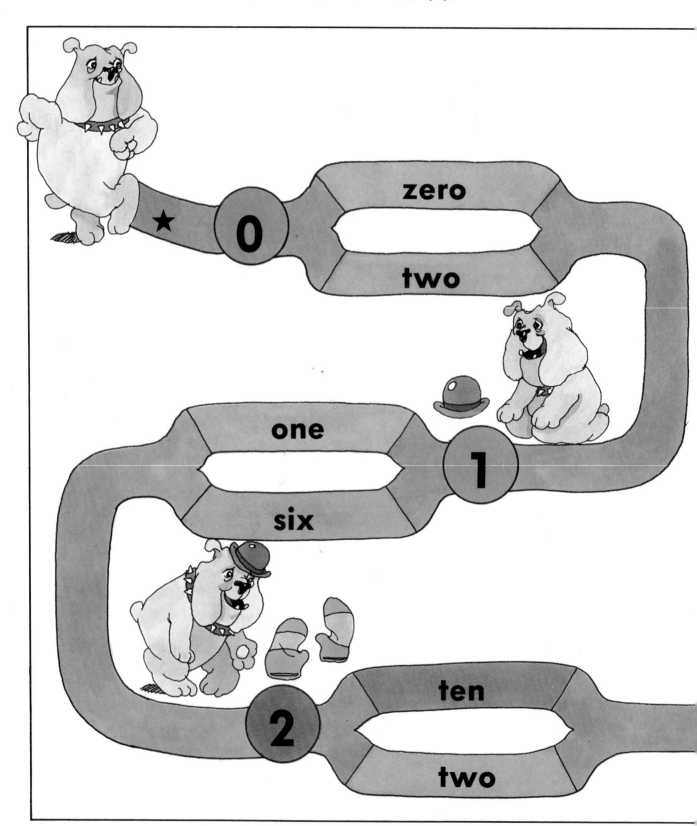

two

five

5

one

four

4

three

eight

3

The Big Bone Hunt

Track **Questron** on the path with number words that match the numbers. Start on the ★.

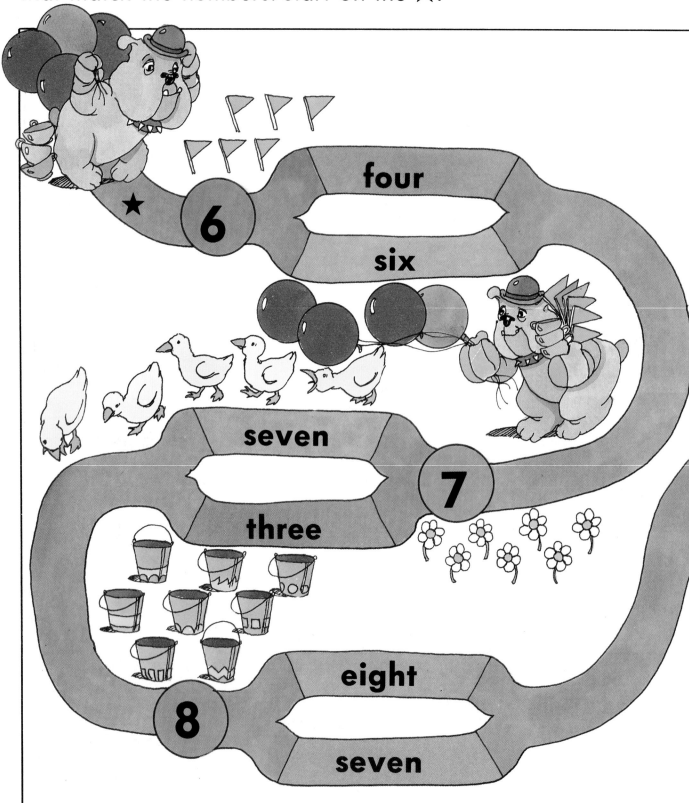

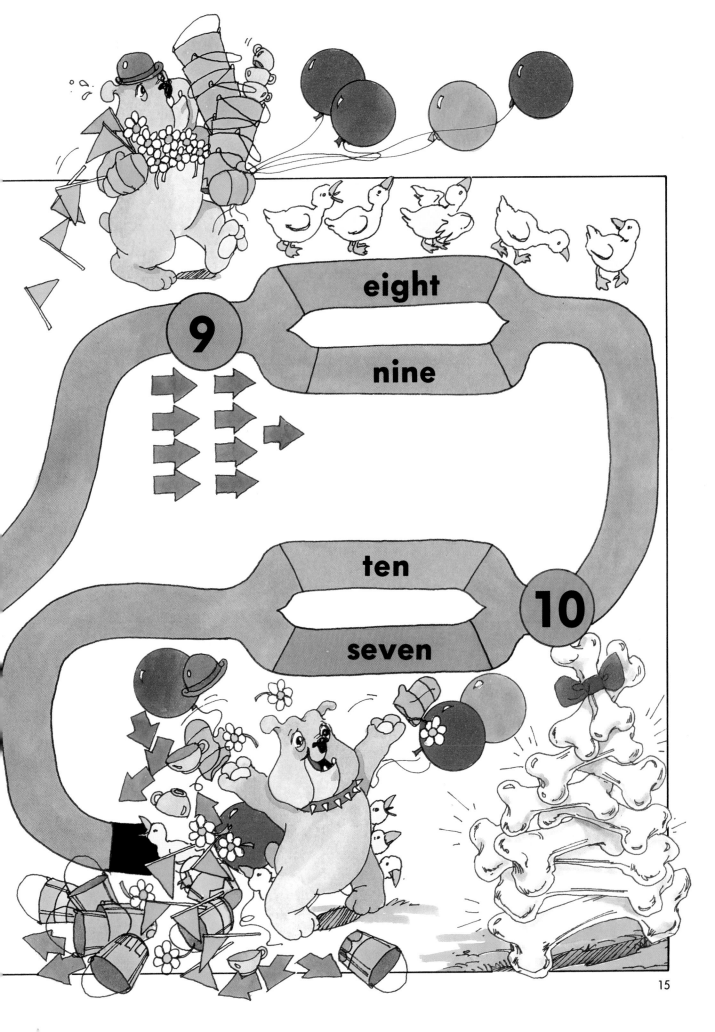

eight

nine

ten

seven

Showtime!

Press **Questron** on the number that matches each number word.

eight

nine

one

five

six

A Happy Home

Press **Questron** on the correct words.

mother

father

tree

mouse

dog

cat

fish

book

father

mother

girl

boy

boy

girl

book

fish

cat

dog

Roll Over, Rover!

Press **Questron** on the word that tells what each dog is doing.

sleep
stand

read
walk

jump
drink

hop
run

stand
sleep

eat

sit

jump

drink

read

jump

eat

sleep

hop

run

Around the Town

Track **Questron** on the path with the words
that match the pictures. Start on the ★.

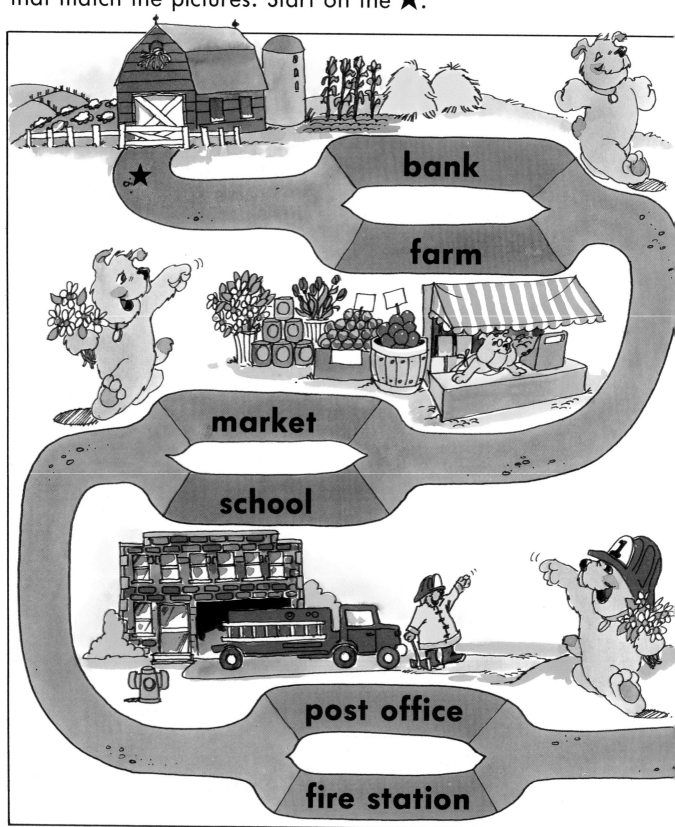

bank

farm

market

school

post office

fire station

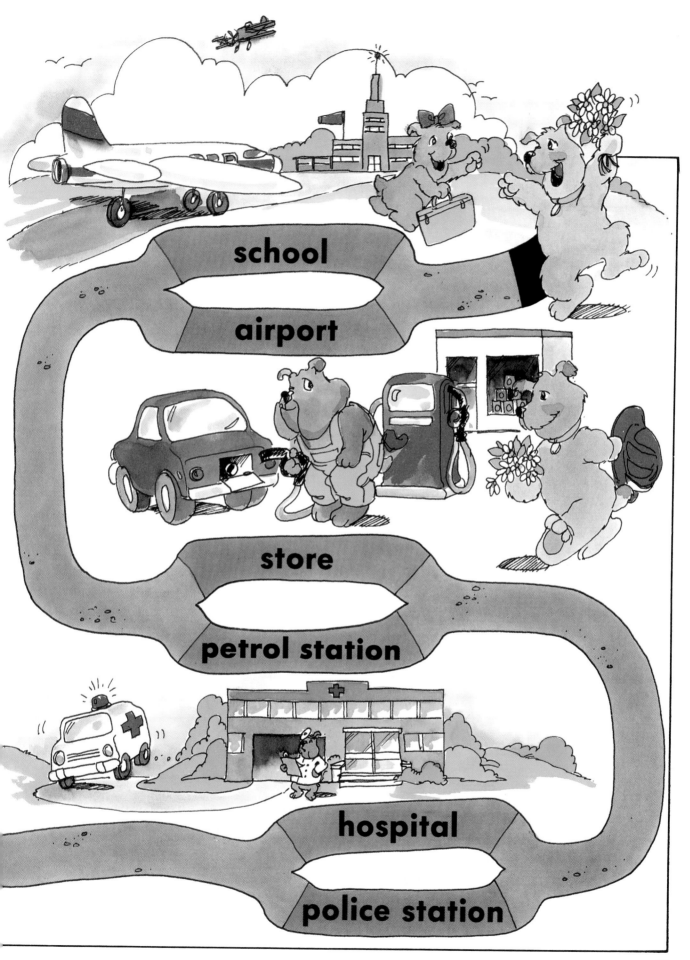

school

airport

store

petrol station

hospital

police station

Playground Pranks

Press **Questron** on the words that tell about the pictures.

At the Zoo

Look at the picture. Press **Questron** on the words that complete each sentence.

I can see | **one** / **two** | .

I can see | **happy** / **sad** | .

I can see | **two** / **three** | .

I can see a **blue** / **brown**  .

I can see a **green** / **red**  .

I can see a **big** / **little**  .

In the Playhouse

Look at the picture. Press **Questron** on the words that complete each sentence.

The **ball** / **doll** is on the  .

The **ball** / **doll** is on the 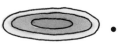 .

The **car** / **doll** is on the ⬭ .

The **hat** / **ball** is on the .

The **boat** / **book** is on the .

The **boat** / **car** is on the .

The **bear** / **boat** is on the .

The **book** / **box** is on the .

Where's the Mouse?

Look at each picture. Track **Questron** to the word that completes each sentence. Start on the ★.

★ I can see a   dog.

cat.

The dog has a friend.

★ The friend is a   mouse.

cat.

★ The dog has a funny   shoe.

hat.

But where is the mouse?

★ The dog looks in the tree.

house.

★ The dog looks under the car.

chair.

Where is the mouse?

★ The mouse is under the boat.

hat.

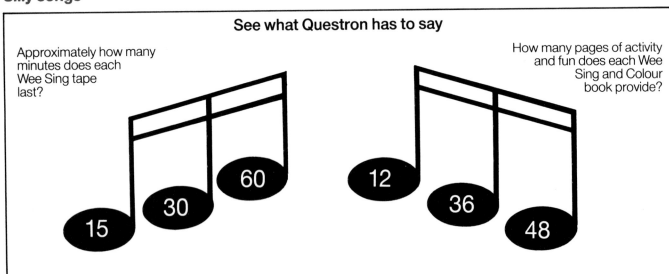